Multiverse of poetic thoughts!

Priyanka Chandgadkar Mishra

Presentation by *BookLeaf Publishing*

Web: www.bookleafpub.com

E-mail: info@bookleafpub.com

ISBN: 978-93-95755-68-9

First edition 2022

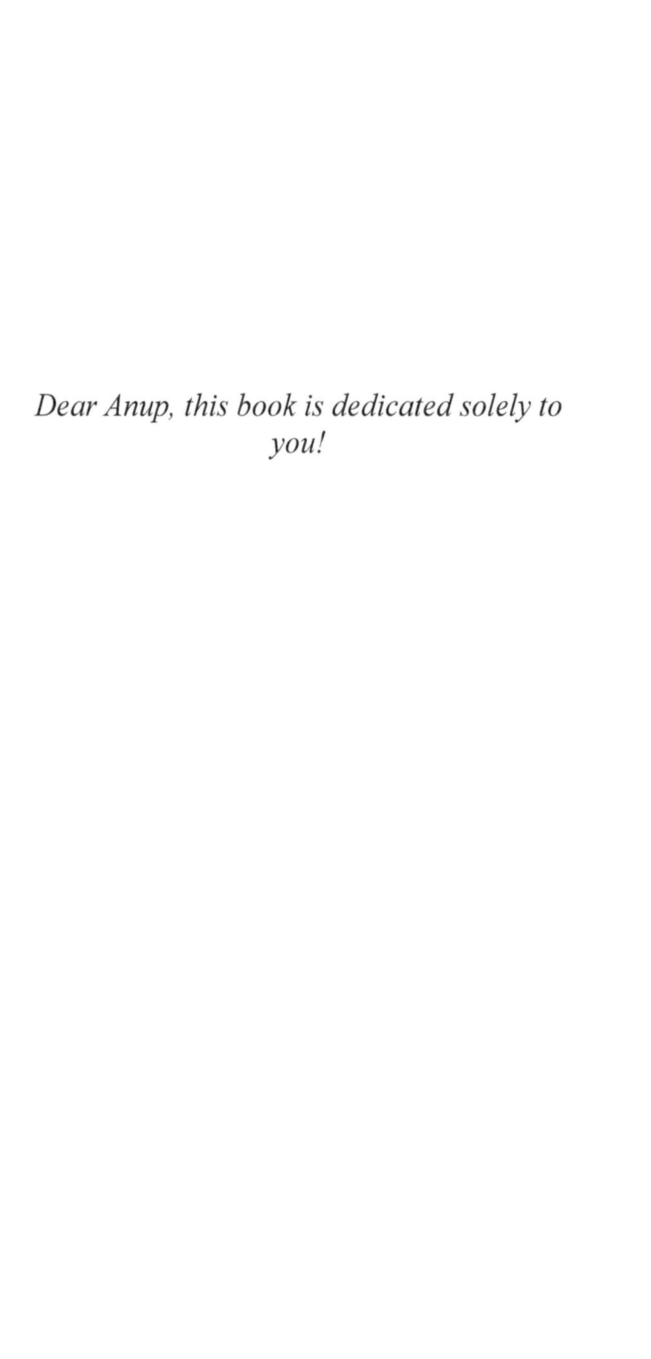

Dear Anup, this book is dedicated solely to you!

ACKNOWLEDGEMENT

I would like to first and foremost thank my husband Anup Mishra, my cheerleader who has supported me since I began writing poems.

I am extremely grateful to my parents (Shubhada, Subhash Chandgadkar) and my in-laws (Shymalata, Kailash Mishra) who have been my biggest partisans & whose blessings have been a key force behind my success.

Finally, I would like to acknowledge my little brother Shubham Chandgadkar, who is my biggest champion, and my sisters-in-law Anjali, Shatabdi, Muskan & brother-in-law Mihir who always make me smile and give me strength.

And last, but not least, I would like to thank all my friends : Abha, Akhila, Vamsi, Robby & Sam who have been pillars of strength and supported me over the years.

Also, thanks to everyone on Book Leaf publishing team.

PREFACE

Creative thoughts are the inspiration for my poems. My fascination with supernatural topics and stories helps me transport into another world and make me write about them.

Some of my poems are inspired by my high hopes, which have always helped me achieve my aspiring dreams.

Almond land

A knock at my door
Woke me from my deep snore
A lady wearing black gown
She held a golden crown..

She blow a shiny powder
I was absorbed inside a boulder
On top..stood a man
He had long hair like a swan..

Loud was his voice ..aura like a diamond
welcomed me with handful of Almond
"Almondland" was the kingdom name..
Finding a queen was its aim..

The man crowned me tiara of flower..
Residing inside were fairies with power
Ruling the realm was like a dream come true
If this is a real world... any clue..?

Abomination

There stood an abandoned house
No one knew the reason of its cause
Some who passed, had seen lights flickering
Some said.. a shadow was lingering
It floats on the red tainted Wall
N screams at midnight 3 to crawl

Scary were the cries..
Gathered the people, to unveil wat resides
The shadow screeched ..
As there was a breach
Chaos begin, as people ran for life,
in this process, a man was left behind!

The shadow latched itself on him
Then, He had a face of grim!
He followed them
and plucked hearts of each one!

The village was abandoned every passing day
It was called "The death's destiny Way"
As you can still hear the voices ..
Of the screams that yell with inverted crosses!

Time Devilry

In the darkness, the clock strikes 3
Travels to the time,
The occultation begins

Where Witches were burnt
Their Cries
Their Pain
Their agony ….
To be reborn….

The Death visited
The time arrived
Dark force had the power
As souls sucked

The Past forwards
To a lonely station
There stood people n children
Witch souls consumed the aura
They sucked children souls

Time flew
Their power grew
Their agony had a curse
No child will be reborn
Without consumed by
Witches , The Blood sucking souls

Existence

In Vicinity of Vast ocean
I question my existence
How enormous are u ocean?
Leading endless expansion

Absorbing Sun's Energy
You are inevitable
Evaporating your tensions
You still smile like a cloud

Greens are your colour
Blues are seldom
Pearls are your bauble
& Corals embellish your charm

You are Home of millions
To sculpt a family
Giving unconditional love
& implore nothing in return!

Dark Souls

A ground full of crosses
Buried in the ground are lifeless bodies
An Undertaker resides there
Listening to screams that despair

Screams that were of murdered souls
Revenge are their ultimate goals
They are trapped on earth
Who are impossible to rebirth

Days pass, their vengeance grows stronger
They start possessing the undertaker
On the nights when moon is darker..
He commits a ruthless murder

Each soul starts attaining its salvation
Only to complete the circle of reincarnation !

Where there is Hope, There is Light !

Darkness annihilates the happiness
It has claws on our dream's fondness
Trying to break the strength rail
It would not listen until you fail
The color of it is Red
With 2 horns on its head
You can't escape its jaws.
That's how it understands your flaws
I am lost in this dark
Its not easy to find a mark
Hope is the only escape
That molds into a positive shape
Oh Look! That light has triggered into fire
I hear darkness, whispering in a mire
With hope, I fight like a conjurer
My aura had the shine of a conqueror
The dark has become white
The sky shines upon me Bright..

Creepy Entrance

Entrance of exquisite flowers,
The roads are decorated with leaves of clovers
Passing the views, my watch has stopped
Oh dear, look the path has blocked!
There comes a fairy,
Grants you 3 wishes to be merry
I wish some happiness, prosperity and wealth
But i forget the health..
She advantages the covet
Allows me to enter with a blanket
I could feel all my desires came true
But I caught a lil flu..
I ignore my instinct's whirled
& believe this is my magical world
I saw some creatures crawling around
They have started to revolve me surround
I fear of my death
Oh fairy, please take all the wealth
I want to be in normal life now
Whom shall I bow?
Please wake me from this dream
Else I would loudly scream..

Pond of Mystery

I am near the pond of fishes
I wanna ask lot of wishes
One of them called me near the pond
I jump inside, only to abscond
The life inside was magnificent.
The aura, the fragrance.. the difference!
A shallow pathway leading to a dark road
I see no one, who could take me thru this fold
I grasp to breath in this water
I have only traveled this far by quarter
A different galaxies I view from the glass
What shall I do, to perform such task?
The portal is at closure
Why did "they" open it at such exposure?
What's secrets this pathway acquire?
Did they choose me for this as a squire?

The Supernatural Entity

Fluid like shadow floating around
I felt a presence, with no one surround
No Odor, no Color.. the eyes popped!
Female spirit, she asked if v could soul swap !
I fainted on floor, as the voice was haunting
She laughed at me, as her intentions were
flaunting
She sat on my chest, pulling my soul
Her appearance had changed into shadow of
dark Kohl
I had my will power as my armor
As Willingness to live, was my only power!
I pushed her aside with my powered arms
She fell like a disarm
The determination is such a strength
It can disassemble any dark entity's
wavelength..!
Believe in yourself, is the emphasized truth
And, makes your body sooth..!

Shining Mermaid

A lake reflecting shiny cloud
I could hear birds chirping so loud
There stood a tree in the middle
It had huge trunk, where leaves were little
Amazed by nature, I desired to feel this tree
There was a small boat with paddles three
I paddled long and reach this place
There stayed a mermaid with a shiny face
She was stunned looking at me
And welcome me as her kind spree
She offered me with a divine drink
Drinking it made me shrink.!!
I was covered with glossy body
And a fish tail which is so sloppy
I was lucky, for the natures Gift
Can you believe you could have such a shift?

The Toad

My car struck on a toad
While I was driving on the road..
I wondered what it had worn..
Heavy his hands were
weak were his legs
Ears were its mouth
& mouth was his ear.
It signaled me to touch its toe
It was too cute to be a foe
I bend to touch..
It grabbed me in its clutch..
It flew up in the sky.
isee along flamingo's fly
I saw the toad turned into an eagle
Its beak had ability to kill lethal
I felt my body had no spine
My skin shining in sunshine
I was breathing with my forked tongue
Just then, I was thrown to flung..
When, I was falling on the riverbed..
Saw my reflection like a snake with hooded
head!
Splash! Was the sound of water
I was back in my car, with my hands shaking in
horror!

Winged Thoughts

Flying was the twinkling object
It floated over my head!
Absorbed me with its opened arms
It looked a spaceship of alien form
Soon, it landed to the peak of a mountain
Mt. Kailash was its name!
In, I was transported
Only to see flying ships n buses floated!
There were creatures like blob
N voices were like throb...
Their eyes were on forehead
Lips were underneath....
"Welcome to the no man's land!"
It came from station that was unmanned
"we who seeded earth
This land is of the future
Time glitch got u here
Don't mention this to any one near!"
I touched my face in fear.
Only to realize I was holding a steer
Quick was i back in my original spot...
Was I dreaming or a passing thought??

Struggles of a Dainty Life!

My dreams have shattered
In my mind, Black clouds have covered
Why Gods are stopping my goal to achieve
I want those to be perceived
I will fight until my last
It would make my body blast
Struggles are everywhere,
Only mine are more than a share!
My potential questions me
Are you a loser to flee?
Be an "eagle" my mind says
These are roads to success, its a phase.!

The Pyramids

Symmetrical is its shape
Single point on its cape...
Pointing towards the Orion's belt it was built
Oh Egyptians! I wonder your quilt.
Did your friends resemble the gods.
As we did not find any constructions flawed..
We see you as the master of afterlife's paths..
No one imagine what journey it would be; will it
be full of wrath?
Why was the pharaoh present?
Deep buried in the sand's scent..
My thoughts seems to be toggled over you.
Please give me wings, I wanna see the view..

A Lone Tree

There stood a lone tree
With its leaves parched
As it was the house of 66 souls
& Inverted laid a chief on its branch
"latch 6 souls a week..else suffer"
Satan recited the goals
The chief searched n hover
To kill n suck Souls
Days passed,
No life could be found near
Satan needed 666 souls to last
From the underground to appear..
The tree evolved
& ingrown its claws..
The souls need to absolved
&opposed the laws..
But, Satan was inevitable
They could not survive its jaws
There stood a lone tree
Searching for its next victim...

What is Mother?

Born with a fairy wings
She loves to swing..!
Believes in Childhood fantasies
Which leads to all contingencies
She is crowned as "princess" by her brood
Matured now, no one viewed
Times have changed from Princess to Queen
With burden of duty, she tends to lean !
She respects all the entitled burden
Without expecting any Guerdon!
Treats this with long lasting smiles
So that her family can achieve success mile!

Ocean LSD

Sand was my bed
Clouds were my shed
Ocean was my music
Birds were playing acoustics
My toe touch a thing
Up I was, saw a still box
Curious was I, pulled the opening string
Swing..! I was inside that block
The terrene was vast
& walls covered with swinging clocks
Each clock unlike other's past
Were Symbolic to different flocks
Buttons were embossed in different granites
Across the clocks, to travel any verse.
Flocks were the planets,
that were from different universe
I pushed the button hue blue
of planet that was skew
Fairies, Flowers, n Trees had a life there
Mermaids had their own kingdom
They questioned my existence
I Dwell from Earth, I said
Hearing, The mother fairy smiled!
She sprinkled a shiny powder..
I was back in the water motions
Relaxing to the sounds of oceans.

Building that stood still

My car had a tire flat,
There crossed a black cat.
It stopped at an abandoned building
Hard was my luck, as it started raining

Building that stood Still!
I stepped in to get some shade
Soon, I felt a feeling of being afraid
The Aura inside was sorrowful
the passage led me to something dreadful

The rooms were filled with beds and tables
They were rusted such, were unstable
Shaking with the thunders outside
I felt my senses had died

Soon then, a light had a flit.
It went across the room and it got lit!
On top was written "Asylum of the Dead Thee"
Entered only to find a dementor, looking at me!
It announced.
"Freshly dead piece she is...
Take her to the Satan, n set her free...
Free to this world but bounded to the
underworld.

Wrap her body in the coffin, begin her
transportation to the netherworld..."

The wrapping process was for a while.
I lay there, with his minions that were patients
that once roam this aisle..
My eyes were stuck at an object far from my
sight.
There laid my body lifeless, like a blight!

Devil Ant

As spring had arrived
It was time for flowers to thrive.
My garden was full of scent
then, I found a flower which was torment..
I asked it, what was wrong?
It hardly smiled..& "POP"… it fell
A Giant butterfly appeared from no-were
It pulled me in. with its wings to lair
I landed in a world of flowers like movie
Saw their faces that were so gloomy
That world was ruled by a "Devil Ant"
Who caged the flowers
With no food and no water..
& screaming chants.
A blue heart shaped flower
Called me near
He gave me a magic potion
To Pour this in the Ants ear
To free them from all this suffer
Courageously I went to Ants throne
Mixed the magic portion with sugar syrup
Oh King..! I said.
Drink this potion from the ear
& the immortality would be near
The ant was tricked.

he was crumbled on the throne
All flowers were set free.. cheering me as their
hero...

The Forbidden Museum

There stood a museum
Burnt and black over a millennium
Went inside I,
Only to find a wall embossed with huge eye
It made me float,
only to absorb me inside a fort
Inside was the underworld
right here on earth...
There stood a life like statue
Of a Beautiful woman,
who had skin of human...
Eyes were like cats
Nails were of lion's n wings like bats
She came in her mortal state
To pounce on my soul..
There she ate my flesh
N gained her youth refreshed
My soul was trapped in cage
Where 99 souls reside
She gained power like Satan...
As, 100 souls made her immortal!!

It was a typical Sunday afternoon, and I was occupied with the mundane household tasks. I was engrossed in completing the stuff like a robot with just one mission in mind - Visiting granny's house as she had been inviting me so long.

Right after finishing my chores, I had a quick hot shower. I hurried to my car carrying the usual backpack. It was around 2 pm when I hit the road. On the way, I was admiring the beautiful mountains, which had a scenic view with the perfect weather. Almost halfway in my journey, the car started to wobble on the highway, I carefully pulled the car aside and cursed myself on being ignorant about the air pressure in tires since it led to flat tire. Moreover, I chose a wrong turn and was isolated since no cars or trucks were nearby to seek help. I picked my cell to call the mechanic and instantaneously the weather transformed! From a bright sunny afternoon to clouds impregnated with rainwater. Then, sharp lightning struck so loud, and it shook me to the bones that I dropped my cell phone. Just then, it started raining heavily. I picked up my cell quickly but found a big crack on it. I looked around to find any help and saw a lonely building a bit away from the road and almost covered in bushes and trees. It appeared to be an old one, distorted and adding to my misery. I could see that the building walls were decorated in Victorian style. It also seemed that it had not been painted in 100 years. I thought I could use the shade and then attempt on getting my cell work. Suddenly, out of nowhere a black cat** crossed the road, startling me. Maybe intimating a possible danger but, my instinct told me not to worry since it's just a superstition and continued to stride to the building.

When I stood in front of the building, its aura reflected an eerie feeling; it somehow felt like it was surrounded by negative energy. Since I was the only human standing, I gathered some courage to enter the creepy building in hope to get some assistance or to notify my granny that I was struck here in a creepy place.

Just then, it started raining tremendously as if the whole area might turn into a river stream. At the time, I was standing in the lobby, my eyes were struck at room to my left where I saw rusted tables, chairs, salt stands, etc. Just as I was about to turn around, another thunder sound took place, which was so loud that I felt my heart skip a beat and my hands trembled. I felt my body numb and thought something is wrong with this place. Then, a mysterious event occurred - a wisp of light rose from the rusted bed and moved across me, leading me to another room. I was drawn to the wisp and saw an entrance that said, "Asylum of the Dead Thee". During my trance, I entered this spooky room where I saw a wraithlike Dark creature staring at me with his neck twisted, it had no face and spoke loudly in crisp voice – "Fresh Dead Piece... transport her body to the underworld, she has no ties to this earth anymore". The ritual was then initiated by his minions- gloomy spirits, who were I feel were once part of the hospital's staff. As my legs trembled in fear, I could not speak, my eyes were fixed on an object on the bed. It was a lifeless form of me where minions were performing rituals. At that moment, I cried out, "Noooo! Suddenly, the clock started ticking 1 pm and my phone rang. It was a dream, wasn't it? ...…… I woke up with my heart pounding like a drum!